Prairie Dogs

Patricia J. Murphy
AR B.L.: 1.9
Points: 0.5                 LG

Grassland Animals

# Prairie Dogs

## by Patricia J. Murphy

Consulting Editor: Gail Saunders-Smith, Ph.D.
Consultant: Marsha A. Sovada, Ph.D., Research Wildlife Biologist
Northern Prairie Wildlife Research Center, U.S. Geological Survey
Jamestown, North Dakota

Capstone
press
Mankato, Minnesota

Pebble Books are published by Capstone Press
151 Good Counsel Drive, P.O. Box 669, Mankato, Minnesota 56002
www.capstonepress.com

1 2 3 4 5 6 09 08 07 06 05 04

*Library of Congress Cataloging-in-Publication Data*
Murphy, Patricia J., 1963–
     Prairie dogs / by Patricia J. Murphy.
     p. cm.—(Grassland animals)
     Summary: Simple text and photographs introduce prairie dogs and their
grasslands habitat.
     Includes bibliographical references (p. 23) and index.
     ISBN 0-7368-2073-6 (hardcover)
     1. Prairie dogs—Juvenile literature. [1. Prairie dogs. 2. Grasslands.] I. Title.
II. Series.
QL737.R68M77 2004
599.36′7—dc22                                                           2003013418

## Note to Parents and Teachers

The Grassland Animals series supports national science standards
related to life science. This book describes and illustrates prairie
dogs. The photographs support early readers in understanding
the text. The repetition of words and phrases helps early readers
learn new words. This book also introduces early readers to
subject-specific vocabulary words, which are defined in the
Glossary. Early readers may need assistance to read some words
and to use the Table of Contents, Glossary, Read More, Internet
Sites, and Index/Word List sections of the book.

# Table of Contents

# Prairie Dogs

Prairie dogs are short, chubby rodents. Rodents are mammals with long front teeth.

Prairie dogs are tan, white, and black. They wag their tails.

Prairie dogs have short legs and long claws. They dig burrows with their claws.

area where prairie dogs live

# Where Prairie Dogs Live

Prairie dogs live on grasslands in North America. Grasslands are large open areas of grass.

Prairie dogs live together in family groups. Many families live together in a prairie dog town.

# What Prairie Dogs Do

Prairie dogs kiss
and groom each other.
They play together.

Prairie dogs munch on grasses, plants, and insects.

Prairie dogs bark to warn each other of danger. Hawks, badgers, and ferrets hunt prairie dogs.

Prairie dogs hide underground in their burrows. They sleep in their burrows at night.

# Glossary

**bark**—a short, loud sound; the prairie dog gets its name from its bark, which sounds like a dog's bark.

**burrow**—a tunnel or a hole in the ground

**grassland**—a large open area of grass; grasslands are also called prairies.

**groom**—to clean oneself; some animals groom themselves.

**mammal**—a warm-blooded animal that has a backbone; mammals have fur or hair; female mammals feed milk to their young.

**munch**—to chew with a crunching sound; prairie dogs munch on grasses that grow around the holes of their burrows; they then can see the surrounding area better.

**rodent**—a mammal with long front teeth; rodents use their teeth to gnaw.

# Read More

**Robinson, W. Wright.** *How Mammals Build Their Amazing Homes.* Animal Architects. Woodbridge, Conn.: Blackbirch Press, 1999.

**Spilsbury, Louise, and Richard Spilsbury.** *A Colony of Prairie Dogs.* Animal Groups. Chicago: Heinemann, 2004.

**Woodward, John.** *Prairie Dogs.* The Secret World Of. Chicago: Raintree, 2003.

# Internet Sites

FactHound offers a safe, fun way to find Internet sites related to this book. All of the sites on FactHound have been researched by our staff.

Here's how:

1. Visit *www.facthound.com*
2. Type in this special code **0736820736** for age-appropriate sites. Or enter a search word related to this book for a more general search.
3. Click on the **Fetch It** button.

FactHound will fetch the best sites for you!

# Index/Word List

bark, 19
burrows,
  9, 21
claws, 9
danger, 19
family, 13
grasslands, 11
groom, 15

hide, 21
hunt, 19
kiss, 15
legs, 9
mammals, 5
munch, 17
North
  America, 11

play, 15
rodents, 5
sleep, 21
tails, 7
teeth, 5
town, 13
underground,
  21

**Word Count: 117**
**Early-Intervention Level: 13**

**Editorial Credits**

Martha E. H. Rustad, editor; Patrick Dentinger, designer; Scott Thoms,
    photo researcher; Karen Risch, product planning editor

**Photo Credits**

Brian Gosewisch, 20
Bruce Coleman Inc./John Shaw, cover
Corbis/Tom Bean, 1
Erwin and Peggy Bauer, 12
Index Stock Imagery/Zefa Visual Media-Germany, 16
McDonald Wildlife Photography/Joe McDonald, 4, 6
Minden Pictures/Jim Brandenburg, 8
Pat and Chuck Blackley, 18
Peggy Patterson/GeoIMAGERY, 14
PhotoDisc Inc., 10

24